# SCREAMS!

# SCREAMS!

YAEL EYLAT-TANAKA

# Copyright

Published by: Yaël Eylat-Tanaka

Tampa, Florida

Email: Yael@pro-wordsmith.net

# Other Books by this author

Diet Proof Your Life

Dreams – Poetry of the Mind

Lake of Silence

The Book of Values

Common Bits of Life

Publish Your Book Using CreateSpace

Publish Your Book on Kindle

Publish Your Book With NOOK Press

Publish Your eBook on Smashwords

Publish Your eBook on BookTango

Publish Your eBook Your Way

Six books of poetry under a pseudonym

# Preface

Fear is an integral part of us creatures. Whether human or otherwise. We are hard-wired to experience fear, and our response to it ranges from freezing to unfettered screams. But screams alone cannot possibly represent the raw anguish, shaking and shivering nerves and sinew, as the body and mind try to deal with an emergency, a life-altering experience that can never be distinguished ...

# CONTENTS

# THE BIRTH

Her screams could be heard on the other floors –
blood curdling, interrupted only by the need to take a breath,
but with every breath she took, she inhaled the unbearably
heavy sweet odor of the ether. A sickening, noxious smell she
could not escape. The mask would be placed around her
mouth and nose, mighty hand vices holding her head still as
she writhed in agony and tried to protest to no avail. She was
strapped down, drugged into submission. Around her,
doctors and nurses scurried about, each attending to another
imperative, going about their business as routine. They had
done this many times before: strap them down, fill them with
sedatives to the point of impotence, then proceed as if their
charge was inert – an unfeeling, insensate blob of flesh.

They had a job to do – extricate another creature from
the body.

Around her, voices vibrated and resounded in her ears
as if they were all talking into loudspeakers. She had been
anesthetized with the maximum dose, yet she remained
conscious. Beneath the veil of sedatives, the futile screams,
the useless protests, the sheer terror. She was at their mercy,
and could not let them know of her suffering.

She screamed, as much from pain as from fear. Control over her own body had been wrenched from her. Chaos all around her. Noise and confusion.

Impossible to escape! Impossible to die.

The ordeal continued unabated. She could not communicate, yet she could hear herself scream. Was it her own voice she heard? Why did they not heed her cries?!

Above her were the four enormous eyes of light glowering down upon her, close enough to touch, yet she could not, blinding her. She could make out the ridges on the casings, the fluorescent sheen that was so close, so nearly touchable ...

And the ether. That awful smell.

He then inserted those tongs, merely adding to the trauma, her passivity, inability to cooperate. She was unable to control her surroundings or her body. She was unwilling to yield, unable to relax, unable to make sense of what was happening. Surrender was impossible. She was their trapped animal, latched down on the sterile table, with those horrible foursome bright light beams hovering over her like menacing sentinels, blinding her, adding to her agitation. The commotion in the room; the instruments of torture – and the chief at her feet, clad in white, enormous goggles for eyes, and a raspy voice barking commands, all around obeying in unison. "Hurry up, Mrs. McGraw, hurry up, we don't have much time," she remembered hearing. "Move over to the table, Mrs. McGraw, hurry up, hurry up …" Hurry up??? She was drugged beyond comprehension; her stupor just this side of death, unable to feel her limbs – and she was being urged to hurry up?? Those words barely registered in her consciousness as they flooded over her, booming over her, around her, into her very being. She only heard herself scream.

She found herself back in her room. Her shrieks still reverberated in her head despite the dullness produced by the drugs. Screams of fear. She did not remember the infant cry – or were her own screams those of the child? The fog was still whirling about her. Her head throbbed. The nightmarish experience rattling her to the core of her being.

They brought her infant son to her, bundled like a cocoon. She marveled at the shock of black hair on that tiny ruddy face, a tiny human being marred by an enormous bloody gash across his brand new forehead. The harsh light at her bedside beamed down on the infant who awoke and began to cry, a tiny, strangled, voiceless, tremulous resentment at being once again jostled to a harsh reality. She could not even hold him. The drugs had not yet dissipated and her arms felt like cotton. But she could remember. And the memories would last a lifetime.

The odor of ether – and those screams.

ಏಲ

# A SIMPLE PROCEDURE

Children are coddled in the United States, but treated as nothing more than little animals in many parts of the world, devoid of opinions, having no choice, without a voice. The "old world" parents surely could not be bothered with a child having an opinion, especially as it related to its health. The child had the sniffles, it was carted off to the doctor; the doctor in turn did what doctors did in those days – probed and plucked, stuck the child with needles – whatever was needed. If the child screamed, that was taken as no more than the sound of the wind through the trees. Like the slaughter of cattle as it is strapped into the murderous steel cage.

She had had her share of throat infections, asthmatic attacks, a litany of childhood illnesses that were inconvenient to the family. At last, when she was 7 or 8, it was decided that her tonsils should be removed. And so began the trauma that would emblazon itself into her memory.

A prickly intelligent child, she had wanted to have some input into her fate, a chance for some decision making in regard her own well-being. That was not to be, however.

Under pretense she was brought to the office of the surgeon, separated from her mother by the assistant, who summarily sat her on his lap, enclosing her between his powerful thighs so as to immobilize her. She tried to resist, but he took both her tiny arms and tucked them tight behind her back, clasping her hands behind her, and then encircled her body with his own arms, belt at the elbows so as to be able to hold her head facing straight to the surgeon. The surgeon, meanwhile, inserted an impossibly large mouth gag into her mouth, and blinded to her screaming protests and attempts to free herself, swung the mask with the awful ether onto her face.

The little girl fell unconscious.

Awakening did not bring relief of pain or fear. Her throat burned, and the promise of unlimited ice cream did little to allay her rage. Yet she kept quiet. Protests meant nothing. Indeed, she had no voice – physically traumatized as she was emotionally bereft of control over her own body.

Her impotent screams can still be heard over the waves of times.

ᏕᎧᏣᎡ

# THE SYMBOL

He had been known among his pals as Tarzan, a nickname he acquired because of his agility in climbing the scorched trees of the region. He was a young man of 21, recently arrived in his adoptive country, enthusiasm firing his mind, an avowed Zionist, hell bent on doing his bit in the formation of a new state. He loved his new home, and the absent amenities, the ruined buildings, bombed out cities and barbed wire did not deter his enthusiasm. He was eager to fight; the impudence of youth.

She remembered him now, on this day of hero worship in her own adopted country, the wreaths placed ceremoniously with great deference and fanfare, at the Tomb of the Unknown Soldier, the president speaking in measured baritones, the cadence of respect and honor for their courage, the fallen of many wars, the ultimate price in service to the country.

But to her, he was the true hero. He did not die in battle, but his life was to be shattered forever. He served his chosen country with the fervor of youth, the longing of the patriot, the sheer folly and recklessness that sometimes reside in the soul of the brave.

A staunch Zionist, he had earned the respect of his fellow soldiers when he risked his life smuggling Jews into Palestine. One by one, he would acquire fishing boats from willing fishermen in his hometown in Africa, load them up with refugees, and row the rickety vessels by the light of the moon. Landing on the beaches was treacherous enough, yet both smugglers and refugees breeched those dangers, as the yearning to be part of the new Jewish state burned in their souls.

He was a strapping, swarthy young man, idealistic as he was fearless. His arrival at the kibbutz was met with a greeting of like-minded young men with an easy readiness to make each other's acquaintance; for in war, social ties are the only succor. They laughed at their austerity, rid the land of rocks and boulders by night, and stood watch under moonlit skies. They sang folk songs and talked of their former homes, even as their new homeland burned and trembled. Always surrounded by snipers and cannons, and the ever-present Arabs who would not relinquish even a square centimeter of what they considered their land, a dispute that traced back to biblical times.

But these kibbutzniks were just as zealous in their quest.

The kibbutzniks fought mightily. Their women bore babies amid the rubble, while their tiny tents provided meager shelter from the scorpions and the hot winds of the desert.

Against this backdrop stretched the lives of these pioneers, one by one sent to the front lines, many never to return.

On that fateful day, he gathered his gear, his knapsack and helmet, lightly kissed his bride and walked out the door. "Shalom, motek," he whispered as he left. She stood at the door, the silence echoing, not daring to wonder when she would see him again. War was everywhere, whistling bullets and detonating bombs. Austerity was a fact of life: water shortages, intermittent electricity, basic necessities of life unavailable. To the 22-year-old young woman, alone in a developing country, away from family, the war machine seemed overwhelming. And she was with child.

To the south, the battle raged with many casualties. Barracks had been erected willy-nilly in the desert, filled with blood-soaked casualties, and the scurrying medics could not keep up with the injured and the dead. Indeed, the battle was so vicious, that burying the dead was impossible. Stench and disease were everywhere. The heat of the desert, the sand storms and the flies only served to test the mettle of the young soldiers. Vastly outnumbered, they managed to hold their own through strategic cunning and sheer determination.

The night skies were hot with the fire of bursting rockets and the continuous volley of rifles and grenades between the camps. The din of the rockets and badly-maintained tanks rumbled by, and the pervasive stench of fuel mingled with the odor of decomposing bodies seared the nostrils. His soul fatigued, his mind on fire, he climbed the Jeep for the southern tip of Palestine, eager to play his part in the fight for her independence.

To the south, the battle raged on, day after scorching day, the weeks stretching on without reprieve from the Arab assaults. On the morning of his second month on duty, when he was awakened abruptly from hard-won slumber to be once again summoned to replace a fallen comrade behind the battle lines. With sleep scratching his eyes and his body aching with weariness, he hopped off his cot, donned his helmet, grabbed his rifle, and ran to his post behind the sacs of sand.

The fusillades screamed by, fireworks lit the sky, yet they held their ground, that tiny sliver of desert at the edge of the sea, refusing to allow the enemy any leeway, resisting the least resignation. No. This land was theirs; their God had made his covenant with their ancestors. It was written …

A screeching, searing pain overwhelmed him and he fell, face into the sand, his mind numb yet raging. Furious unformed thoughts sped by, mingled with fire and torment, unconsciousness and impotence overtaking him, as he swam in dizzy screams, unable to make sense of his surroundings. Then the voices of his comrades became more distinct, and he knew he was being rushed to – where? What were they doing? Where were they going?

His screams mingled with the horrors of the war, the chaos and bombs, the desert dust and searing heat. A grenade had detonated nearby, seriously injuring him, and now he was lying prostrate, impotent, at the mercy of the medics who were preparing to maim him. Him, a young man, full of the vigor of youth. His very life now lay in ruins, for how would he carry out his life mission. Around him scurried soldiers and medics, some shouting orders, complete pandemonium in this make-shift tent at the edge of battle, bloodied bodies everywhere, moans from the injured, screaming protests from the wounded, and the sheer mettle required of the young men and women who tended to them. There was no room for tears and regrets – there was only bedlam.

He would know soon enough.

His body was shaken on the gurney as they rushed him to the medics' tent. There they lay him on a table while the young surgeon in training assessed the situation. Only one course of action was available – it would save his life, but would take his leg. In the field of battle, only the most expedient recourses could be employed. Amenities were few, choices even fewer. And so the saw was prepared, bloodied and unsanitary, while his buddies held him down. His ear-piercing objections and screams filled the air.

A daughter was born shortly thereafter.

* * *

Many years later, his daughter asked him, "Did you ever think of me?"

"You were the symbol of my youth," he replied.

www.ingramcontent.com/pod-product-compliance
Lightning Source LLC
Chambersburg PA
CBHW072254310526
45795CB00011B/1134